First American edition published 1983 by Prentice-Hall Books for Young Readers
A Division of Simon & Schuster, Inc., Simon & Schuster Building
Rockefeller Center, 1230 Avenue of the Americas, New York, NY 10020
Originated by J. M. Dent & Sons Ltd, First published in Great Britain 1983
Copyright © 1983 by Jane Miller, All rights reserved
Phototypeset in Great Britain by Midford Typesetting
Printed and bound in Singapore by Tien Wah Press Pte
The author would like to thank the following in particular
for their invaluable help and assistance with this book:
Jean Brooker   G. C. Hartley of Copas Bros. Cookham, Berks
Elizabeth McWean   Hazel and Nick Round   Whitbread & Co. Ltd.

10 9 8 7 6 5 4 3 2 1

10 9 8 7 6 5 4 3 2 1 pbk

Prentice-Hall Books for Young Readers is a trademark of Simon & Schuster, Inc.

Library of Congress Cataloging in Publication Data
Miller, Jane.
Summary: Introduces simple number concepts using
color photographs of favorite farm animals.
1. Counting—Juvenile literature.   [1. Counting.
2. Domestic animals—Pictorial works]   1. Title.
OA113.M536   1983   513'.2   [E]   82-21622
ISBN 0-13-304790-3   ISBN 0-13-304809-8 pbk

For Patricia Blake

Farm Counting Book

JANE MILLER

Prentice-Hall Books for Young Readers

A Division of Simon & Schuster, Inc.

New York

1

one kitten

2
two lambs

3

three horses

4

four pigs

5
five cows

6

six dogs

7

seven ducks

8

eight swans

9

nine horseshoes

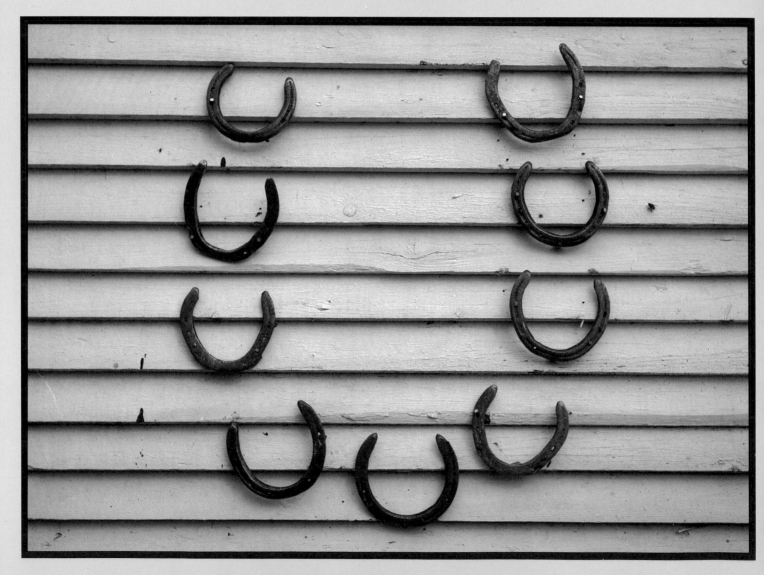

10

ten geese

Here is 1 puppy –

and 1 bed for the puppy.

How many cats are there?

Is there a bowl of milk for each cat?

Here are 3 cows.

1 donkey   1 foal   1 goat

3 animals altogether

How many ducks can you count?
How many white ducks are there?
Are there more white ducks than brown ducks?

How many piglets are there in this litter?

How many chicks are there in this brood?

How many geese can you see?

How many sheep are there?

How many ponies are there?

How many foals?

How many strawberries are there in this picture?

Are there the same number of strawberries in this picture?

Can you count how many eggs there are in this picture?

Following her highly successful "Farm Alphabet Book" —
hailed by "The Guardian" as 'a visual delight' — comes Jane
Miller's "Farm Counting Book", also illustrated with full-
colour photographs. Born and brought up in Australia,
Jane Miller started taking photographs at the age of ten,
and even at that age processed them herself. After living in
Thailand, India and the United States, she became a free-
lance photographer and began to work professionally. She
has been based in England since 1947, and her
photographs appear widely in magazines, newspapers
and books, as well as on calendars and greeting cards.